This Book Belongs To:

_____

_____

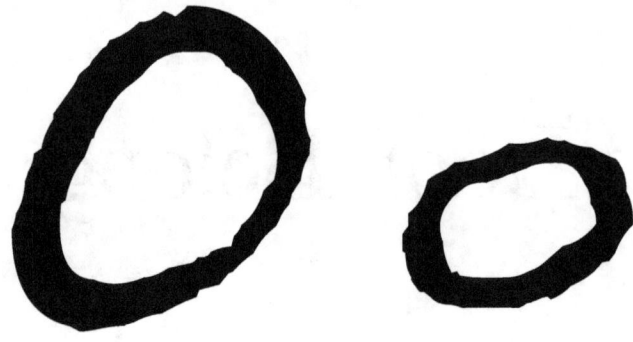

Octopus Okra

Who did you help today?

Cc

Chocolate Carrot

What made you smile today?

Yy

Yoghurt Yams

How do you show love to your family?

Hh

Haddock Ham

What did you learn that made you feel proud today?

Dd

Durian Donut

What makes you feel happy?

Gg

Grape Gnocchi ♥

How do you show gratitude?

Zz

Zucchini Zuccotto

How do you eat your favorite dessert?

Avocado Asparagus

What are you thankful for?

P p

Pineapple Panfish

What made you laugh today?

Ii

Idiyappam Ice cream

What was the best part of your day?

Uthappam Uszka

Who comforts you when you feel blue?

Jambalaya Jam

What hobby do you want to learn?

Xigua Xiphias

How do you like to celebrate?

Ee

Eggplant Empanadas

How do you cheer yourself up?

Ss

Squid Scones

How can you make more friends?

L l

Liver Lobster

What is the nicest thing anyone has
said about you?

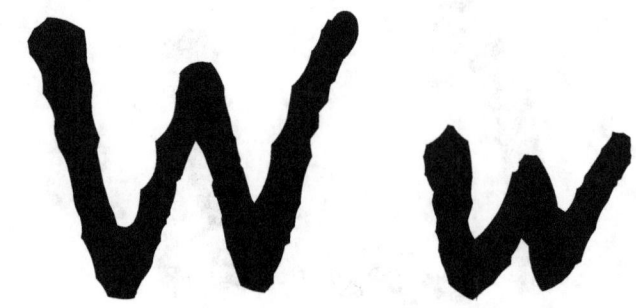

Walnut Wontons

What goals do you have?

Mm

Mackerel Muffins

What toys are you thankful for?

Quiche Quesadillas

Who are your favorite people?

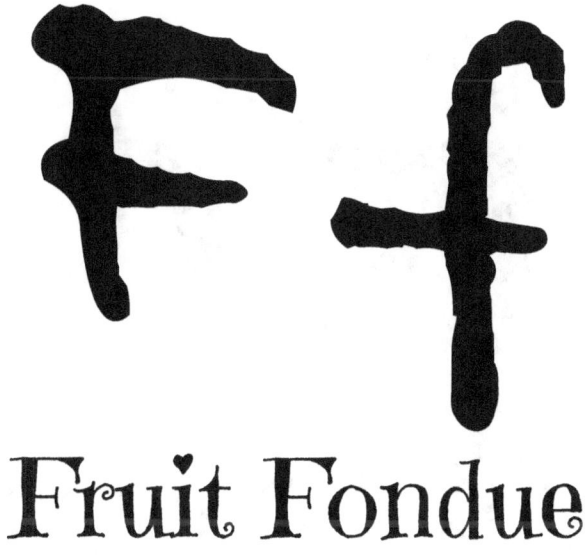

Fruit Fondue

What is something you are looking forward to?

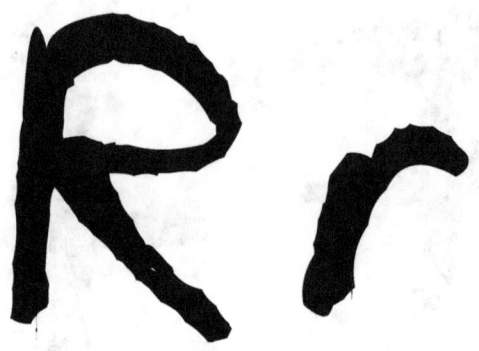

Radish Ratatouille

What can you do to improve
yourself?

V v

Vla Vindaloo

What skill did you practice today?

Nectarine Noodles

What are your favorite colors?

T t

Tangerine Tofu

What did you achieve today?

Bb

Blueberry Burrito

Who do you want to thank today?